MEMORIAL

ALSO BY ALICE OSWALD

POETRY

The Thing in the Gap-Stone Stile

Dart

Woods Etc.

A Sleepwalk on the Severn

Weeds and Wild Flowers

EDITOR

The Thunder Mutters: 101 Poems for the Planet

Thomas Wyatt: Selected Poems

MEMORIAL

A VERSION OF HOMER'S *Iliad*

ALICE OSWALD

W. W. NORTON & COMPANY

NEW YORK   LONDON

For information about permission to reproduce selections from
this book, write to Permissions, W. W. Norton & Company, Inc.,
500 Fifth Avenue, New York, NY 10110

For information about special discounts for bulk purchases,
please contact W. W. Norton Special Sales at
specialsales@wwnorton.com or 800-233-4830

Manufacturing by Courier Westford
Production manager: Louise Mattarelliano

Library of Congress Cataloging-in-Publication Data

Oswald, Alice, 1966–
Memorial : a version of Homer's Iliad / Alice Oswald ; with an afterword by
Eavan Boland. — 1st American ed.
p. cm.
"First published in 2011 in Great Britain by Faber and Faber Limited
under the title MEMORIAL: An Excavation of the Iliad"—T.p. verso.
ISBN 978-0-393-08867-0 (hardcover)
I. Homer. Iliad—Poetry. 2. Achilles (Greek mythology)—Poetry.
3. Trojan War—Poetry. I. Title.
PR6065.S98M46 2012
821'.914—dc23
                                      2012022791

W. W. Norton & Company, Inc.,
500 Fifth Avenue, New York, N.Y. 10110
www.wwnorton.com

W. W. Norton & Company Ltd.,
Castle House, 75/76 Wells Street, London W1T 3QT

1 2 3 4 5 6 7 8 9 0

Acknowledgments

Very many thanks to: Peter Oswald, Laura Beatty and the Keens, Sheila Hooker, Jules Cashford, Rupert Smith, Paul Keegan, Kevin Mount, Joe Richards, Iris Milward, Jo Larsen, Jerome Fletcher, Philip Franses, Minni Jain, Warwick Gould and the staff at Senate House Library, University of London – and Homer.

This is a translation of the *Iliad*'s atmosphere, not its story. Matthew Arnold (and almost everyone ever since) has praised the *Iliad* for its 'nobility'. But ancient critics praised its *'enargeia'*, which means something like 'bright unbearable reality'. It's the word used when gods come to earth not in disguise but as themselves. This version, trying to retrieve the poem's *enargeia*, takes away its narrative, as you might lift the roof off a church in order to remember what you're worshipping. What's left is a bipolar poem made of similes and short biographies of soldiers, both of which derive (I think) from distinct poetic sources: the similes from pastoral lyric (you can tell this because their metre is sometimes compressed as if it originally formed part of a lyric poem); the biographies from the Greek tradition of lament poetry.

There are accounts of Greek lament in both the *Iliad* and the *Odyssey*. When a corpse was layed out, a professional poet (someone like Homer) led the mourning and was antiphonally answered by women offering personal accounts of the deceased. I like to think that the stories of individual soldiers recorded in the *Iliad* might be recollections of these laments, woven into the narrative by poets who regularly performed both high epic and choral lyric poetry.

The *Iliad* is a vocative poem. Perhaps even (in common with lament) it is invocative. It always addresses Patroclus as 'you', as if speaking directly to the dead. This translation presents the whole poem as a kind of oral cemetery – in the aftermath of the Trojan War, an attempt to remember people's names and lives without the use of writing. I hope it doesn't need too much context. I hope it will have its own coherence as a series of memories and similes laid side by side: an antiphonal account of man in his world.

I should add a note about my attitude to the printed *Iliad*. My 'biographies' are paraphrases of the Greek, my similes are translations. However, my approach to translation is fairly irreverent. I work closely with the Greek, but instead of carrying the words over into English, I use them as openings through which to see what Homer was looking at. I write through the Greek, not from it — aiming for translucence rather than translation. I think this method, as well as my reckless dismissal of seven-eighths of the poem, is compatible with the spirit of oral poetry, which was never stable but always adapting itself to a new audience, as if its language, unlike written language, was still alive and kicking.

MEMORIAL

PROTESILAUS

ECHEPOLUS

ELEPHENOR

SIMOISIUS

LEUKOS

DEMOCOON

DIORES

PIROUS

PHEGEUS

IDAEUS

ODIOS

PHAESTUS

SCAMANDRIUS

PHERECLES

PEDAEUS

HYPSENOR

ASTYNOOS

HYPEIRON

ABAS

POLYIDOS

XANTHUS

THOON

ECHEMMON

CHROMIUS

PANDARUS

DEICOON

ORSILOCHUS

I

CRETHON

PYLAEMENES

MYDON

MENESTHES

ANCHIALOS

AMPHIUS

TLEPOLEMOS

COERANUS

CHROMIUS

ALCASTOR

ALCANDER

HALIUS

PYRTANIS

NOEMON

TEUTHRAS

ORESTES

TRECHUS

OENOMAUS

HELENUS

ORESBIUS

PERIPHAS

ACAMAS

AXYLUS

CALESIUS

PEDASUS

AESEPUS

ASTYALOS

PIDUTES

ARETAON

ANTILOCHUS

ELATUS

PHYLAKOS

MELANTHIUS

ADRESTUS

MENESTHIUS

IPHINOUS

ENIOPEUS

AGELAOS

ORSILOCHUS

ORMENUS

OPHELESTES

DAETOR

CHROMIUS

LYCOPHONTES

AMOPAON

MELANIPPUS

GORGYTHION

ARCHEPTOLEMOS

DOLON

RHESUS

ISOS

ANTIPHOS

PEISANDER

HIPPOLOCHUS

IPHIDAMAS

COON

ASAEUS

AUTONOOS

OPITES

DOLOPS

OPHELTIUS

AGELAOS

AESYMNUS

ORUS

HIPPONOUS

THYMBRAIUS

MOLION

ADRESTUS

AMPHIUS

HIPPODAMOS

HYPEIROCHOS

AGASTRAPHUS

THOON

ENNOMUS

CHERSIDAMAS

SOCUS

CHAROPS

DORYCLES

PANDOCUS

LYSANDER

PYRASUS

PYLARTES

APISAON

DAMASOS

PYLON

ORMENOS

HIPPOMACHOS

ANTIPHATES

MENON

IAMENOS

ORESTES

EPICLES

IMBRIOS

AMPHIMACHOS

OTHRYON

ASIUS

ALCATHOUS

OINOMAOS

ASKALAPHOS

APHAREUS

THOON

ANTILOCHUS

DEIPUROS

PEISANDER

HARPALION

EUCHENOR

SATNIUS

PROTHOENOR

ARCHELOCHUS

PROMACHUS

ILIONEUS

STICHIUS

ARCESILAUS

MEDON

IASUS

MECISTEUS

ECHIUS

CLONIUS

DEIOCHUS

KALETOR

LYKOPHRON

KLEITOS

SCHEDIOS

LAODAMAS

OTOS

KROISMOS

DOLOPS

MELANIPPUS

PERIPHETOS

PURAICHMES

AREILYCUS

THOAS

AMPHICLUS

ATUMNIOS

MARIS

KLEOBULOS

LYKON

AKAMAS

ERYMAS

PRONOOS

THESTOR

ERYLAOS

ERYMAS

AMPHOTERUS

EPALTES

TLEPOLEMOS

ECHIOS

PURIS

IPHES

EUIPPOS

POLYMELOS

THRASYMELOS

PEDASUS

SARPEDON

EPIGEUS

BATHYCLES

LAOGONUS

PATROCLUS

EUPHORBAS

HIPPOTHOUS

SCHEDIUS

PHORCYS

LEOCRITUS

APISAON

ARETUS

PODES

KOIRANUS

IPHITUS

DEMOLEON

HIPPODAMAS

POLYDORUS

DRYOPS

DEMUCHUS

LAOGONUS

DARDANUS

TROS

MULIUS

RHIGMOS

LYCAON

THERSILOCHUS

MYDON

ASTYPYLOS

MNESIUS

THRASIUS

AINIOS

OPHELESTES

HECTOR

The first to die was PROTESILAUS
A focused man who hurried to darkness
With forty black ships leaving the land behind
Men sailed with him from those flower-lit cliffs
Where the grass gives growth to everything
Pyrasus   Iton   Pteleus   Antron
He died in mid-air jumping to be first ashore
There was his house half-built
His wife rushed out clawing her face
Podarcus his altogether less impressive brother
Took over command but that was long ago
He's been in the black earth now for thousands of years

Like a wind-murmur
Begins a rumour of waves
One long note getting louder
The water breathes a deep sigh
Like a land-ripple
When the west wind runs through a field
Wishing and searching
Nothing to be found
The corn-stalks shake their green heads

Like a wind-murmur
Begins a rumour of waves
One long note getting louder
The water breathes a deep sigh
Like a land-ripple
When the west wind runs through a field
Wishing and searching
Nothing to be found
The corn-stalks shake their green heads

ECHEPOLUS a perfect fighter
Always ahead of his men
Known for his cold seed-like concentration
Moving out and out among the spears
Died at the hands of Antilochus
You can see the hole in the helmet just under the ridge
Where the point of the blade passed through
And stuck in his forehead
Letting the darkness leak down over his eyes

ELEPHENOR from Euboea in command of forty ships
Son of Chalcodon nothing is known of his mother
Died dragging the corpse of Echepolus
A little flash of flesh showing under the shield as he bent
Agenor stabbed him in the ninth year of the war
He wore his hair long at the back

Like leaves
Sometimes they light their green flames
And are fed by the earth
And sometimes it snuffs them out

Like leaves
Sometimes they light their green flames
And are fed by the earth
And sometimes it snuffs them out

SIMOISIUS born on the banks of the Simois
Son of Anthemion his mother a shepherdess
Still following the sheep when she gave birth
A lithe and promising young man unmarried
Was met by Ajax in the ninth year of the war
And died full tilt running onto his spear
The point passed clean through the nipple
And came out through the shoulderblade
He collapsed instantly an unspeakable sorrow to his parents

And LEUKOS friend of Odysseus
Little is known of him except his death

And someone's face pierced like a piece of fruit
That was Priam's son unlucky man
Who made his living in the horse country
North of Troy he was stepping backwards

When the darkness hit him with a dull clang
His name was DEMOCOON

Like a man steps back
Seeing a snake almost under his foot
In a heathery hollow
The fear flutters his knees it
Sucks him white he steps back

Like a man steps back
Seeing a snake almost under his foot
In a heathery hollow
The fear flutters his knees it
Sucks him white he steps back

DIORES son of Amarinceus
Struck by a flying flint
Died in a puddle of his own guts
Slammed down into mud he lies
With his arms stretched out to his friends
And PIROUS the Thracian
You can tell him by his knotted hair
Lies alongside him
He killed him and was killed
There seem to be black flints
Everywhere a man steps

Like through the jointed grass
The long-stemmed deer
Almost vanishes
But a hound has already found her flattened tracks
And he's running through the fields towards her

Like through the jointed grass
The long-stemmed deer
Almost vanishes
But a hound has already found her flattened tracks
And he's running through the fields towards her

The priest of Hephaestus
Hot-faced from staring at flames
Prayed every morning the same prayer
Please god respect my status
Protect my sons PHEGEUS and IDAEUS
Calm down their horses lift them
Out of the fight as light as ash
Hephaestus heard him but he couldn't
Hold those bold boys back
Riding over the battlefield too fast
They met a flying spear
And like a lift door closing
Inexplicable Hephaestus
Whisked one of them away
And the other died

What happened to that man from Alybe far away in the east
What happened to ODIOS what happened to PHAESTUS
He came from Tarne where the soil is loose and crumbly

Like snow falling like snow
When the living winds shake the clouds into pieces
Like flutters of silence hurrying down
To put a stop to the earth at her leafwork

Like snow falling like snow
When the living winds shake the clouds into pieces
Like flutters of silence hurrying down
To put a stop to the earth at her leafwork

SCAMANDRIUS the hunter
Knew every deer in the woods
He used to hear the voice of Artemis
Calling out to him in the lunar
No man's land of the mountains
She taught him to track her animals
But impartial death has killed the killer
Now Artemis with all her arrows can't help him up
His accurate firing arm is useless
Menelaus stabbed him
One spear-thrust through the shoulders
And the point came out through the ribs
His father was Strophius

Like when a mother is rushing
And a little girl clings to her clothes
Wants help wants arms
Won't let her walk
Like staring up at that tower of adulthood
Wanting to be light again
Wanting this whole problem of living to be lifted
And carried on a hip

Like when a mother is rushing
And a little girl clings to her clothes
Wants help wants arms
Won't let her walk
Like staring up at that tower of adulthood
Wanting to be light again
Wanting this whole problem of living to be lifted
And carried on a hip

Beloved of Athene PHERECLES son of Harmion
Brilliant with his hands and born of a long line of craftsmen
It was he who built the cursed fleet of Paris
Little knowing it was his own death boat
Died on his knees screaming
Meriones speared him in the buttock
And the point pierced him in the bladder

And PEDAEUS the unwanted one
The mistake of his father's mistress
Felt the hot shock in his neck of Meges' spear
Unswallowable sore throat of metal in his mouth
Right through his teeth
He died biting down on the spearhead

Like suddenly it thunders
And a stormwind rushes down
And roars into the sea's ears
And the curves of many white-patched waves
Run this way and that way

Like suddenly it thunders
And a stormwind rushes down
And roars into the sea's ears
And the curves of many white-patched waves
Run this way and that way

Brave HYPSENOR the stump of whose hand
Lies somewhere on the battlefield
He was the son of Dolopion the river-priest
Now he belongs to a great red emptiness

Like when the rainy fog pulls down its hood on the mountains
Misery for the herdsman better than night for the thief
You can see no further than you can throw a stone

Like when the rainy fog pulls down its hood on the mountains
Misery for the herdsman better than night for the thief
You can see no further than you can throw a stone

Diomedes a madman a terrible numbness
Turned inside-out and taking over everything
Killed ASTYNOOS killed HYPEIRON
Killed ABAS and POLYIDOS
Their father could tell the future
But he never prophesied that
Killed XANTHUS and THOON
Both tall men but their father
Was a little wisp of worries
Waiting at home what could he do
Now all his savings will go to other people's children
Now he will have to live off nothing
But his sons' names meanwhile Diomedes
With his eyes peeled down to their see-through stones
Seeing through everything to its inner emptiness
Killed ECHEMMON killed CHROMIUS
Tin-opened them out of their armour
And took for himself their high-stepping horses

Like the high unescapable eye
Of the eagle
Under whose beam
The shadow-swift hare can't hide
Pressed flat to the floor

Of a leafy wood
That loitering eye looks once
And kills

Like the high unescapable eye
Of the eagle
Under whose beam
The shadow-swift hare can't hide
Pressed flat to the floor
Of a leafy wood
That loitering eye looks once
And kills

PANDARUS son of Lycaon had a wife at home
In his high-roofed house in the foothills of Ida
He was captain of Zelea and he and his men
Used to drink the black raw water from the river
He was a rich man a master bowman
Eleven war cars in his stables brand new beautifully made
With rugs and thoroughbred horses
He couldn't bear to risk them in the War
He went on foot to Troy with nothing but his bow
But that was no good to him
The arrows kept flying off at angles
If I ever get home he said
And see my wife and my high-roofed house
May a stranger cut off my head if I don't
Smash this bow and throw it with my own hands

Into the fire it has proved such a nothingness
But he climbed up nevertheless next to Aeneas
He charged at Diomedes and a spear
Thrown by Diomedes pushed hard in by Athene
Hit him between the eyes it split-second
Splintered his teeth cut through his tongue broke off his jaw
And came out clean through the chin

Like an oak tree struck by lightning
Throws up its arms and burns
Terrifying for a man out walking
To smell that sulphur smell
And see the fields flickering ahead of him
Lit up blue by the strangeness of god

Like an oak tree struck by lightning
Throws up its arms and burns
Terrifying for a man out walking
To smell that sulphur smell
And see the fields flickering ahead of him
Lit up blue by the strangeness of god

DEICOON the Trojan
Was too eager too heroic
He found praise yes
But also death

Like snow falls quickly from god to the ground
When the north wind blows down the heavens

Like snow falls quickly from god to the ground
When the north wind blows down the heavens

ORSILOCHUS and CRETHON grew restless
They had shallow stony eyes
Always staring at the pulling sea
And they were the grandsons of a river
Famous Alpheus whose muscular waters
Wind round Pylos
But those cold blue arms couldn't keep them
As soon as they were old enough
They took a ship to Troy their story
Finishes here in darkness

What happened to PYLAEMENES
He came from the Black Sea those dusty plains
That bring forth mules and loud men
His heart was made of coarse cloth
And his manners were loose like old sacking
He was a great captain but Menelaus killed him
And his driver MYDON in the act of turning his horses
Was killed by Antilochus

Like two mules on a shaly path in the mountains
Carrying a huge roof truss or the beam of a boat

Go on mile after mile giving it their willingness
Until the effort breaks their strength

Like two mules on a shaly path in the mountains
Carrying a huge roof truss or the beam of a boat
Go on mile after mile giving it their willingness
Until the effort breaks their strength

And
MENESTHES
ANCHIALOS
AMPHIUS
TLEPOLEMOS
COERANUS
CHROMIUS
ALCASTOR
ALCANDER
HALIUS
PYRTANIS
NOEMON
TEUTHRAS
ORESTES
TRECHUS
OENOMAUS
HELENUS
ORESBIUS
PERIPHAS
And

ACAMAS a massive man best fighter in Thrace
Came over the choppy tides of the Hellespont
And almost instantly took a blow on his helmet
The spear pressed through to his skull
Tipped with darkness
It was Ajax who stopped him

Like that slow-motion moment
When a woman weighs the wool
Her poor old spider hands
Work all night spinning a living for her children
And then she stops
She soothes the scales to a standstill

Like that slow-motion moment
When a woman weighs the wool
Her poor old spider hands
Work all night spinning a living for her children
And then she stops
She soothes the scales to a standstill

AXYLUS son of Teuthras
Lived all his life in the lovely harbour of Arisbe
Looking down at the Hellespont
Everyone knew that plump man
Sitting on the step with his door wide open
He who so loved his friends

Died side by side with CALESIUS
In a daze of loneliness
Their conversation unfinished

Like the hawk of the hills the perfect killer
Easily outflies the clattering dove
She dips away but he follows he ripples
He hangs his black hooks over her
And snares her with a thin cry
In praise of her softness

Like the hawk of the hills the perfect killer
Easily outflies the clattering dove
She dips away but he follows he ripples
He hangs his black hooks over her
And snares her with a thin cry
In praise of her softness

There was a blue pool who loved her loneliness
Lay on her stones clear-eyed staring at trees
Her name was Abarbarea
A young man found her in the hills
He took one look at her shivering freshness
And stripped off his clothes
In the middle of his astonished sheep
He jumped off a rock right into her arms
And from that quick fling there were two children

PEDASUS and AESEPUS
They died at Troy on the same day

Like when a ditch-maker takes a mattock to water
To cut it loose from its clods at first
It's just a secret trickle under nettles
But then the pebbles shout out water
And it runs downhill calling to his crops and orchards
Leaving him staring

Like when a ditch-maker takes a mattock to water
To cut it loose from its clods at first
It's just a secret trickle under nettles
But then the pebbles shout out water
And it runs downhill calling to his crops and orchards
Leaving him staring

ASTYALOS
PIDUTES
ARETAON
The flash of a spear
Woke them with a jolt
And
ANTILOCHUS
ELATUS
PHYLAKOS
MELANTHIUS

Like when god keeps the night awake with lightning
And the sky jumps into readiness for a huge rainstorm
And sometimes hail or snow when blizzards wander in the fields

Like when god keeps the night awake with lightning
And the sky jumps into readiness for a huge rainstorm
And sometimes hail or snow when blizzards wander in the fields

ADRESTUS almost survived it was horrible
To hear the hoof-kicking struggle of his horses
Tangled on a tamarisk branch
The cart cracked the man tipped headfirst forwards
And landed on his mouth in the dust
And there instantly stood Menelaus
A sundial moving over his last moments
With a long shadowing spear
Take me alive said Adrestus
I'll give you everything gold bronze iron
My father is a rich man take me alive
But Agamemnon heard him
Weakness what is this weakness Menelaus
Don't tell me you love these men
With their impeccable wife-thief manners
A death-curse on all of them kill them all
Even the unborn ones in their mothers' bellies
Be uncried for unburied
And that was the earth's moment
That was the death of Adrestus

Like a good axe in good hands
Finds out the secret of wood and splits it open
When a man for example cuts out timbers for a boat
And his axe is an iron decision swinging his arm

Like a good axe in good hands
Finds out the secret of wood and splits it open
When a man for example cuts out timbers for a boat
And his axe is an iron decision swinging his arm

MENESTHIUS the only son of big-eyed Phylomedusa
Came overland to Troy not quite knowing why
Until he met Paris running in a love-rage towards him
With the smell of Helen still on his hands

Like a rainbow shining a warning to the world
A bright banner of disruption hung above the fields
Meaning war perhaps or maybe just a summer storm
So that everyone stops work and looks up and the flocks
                        grow restless

Like a rainbow shining a warning to the world
A bright banner of disruption hung above the fields
Meaning war perhaps or maybe just a summer storm
So that everyone stops work and looks up and the flocks
                        grow restless

Another man springing into his chariot
Felt a blow on his shoulder and dropped
Like a leaf from a topmost twig
His name was IPHINOUS

And ENIOPEUS with high hopes
Drove Hector into battle
Into the terrifying anti-world of the wounded
The wheels kept slewing over bodies
But he held tight he was good with horses
Until a spear shocked him in the nipple
He vanished backwards and hit the ground under their hooves
Clang his soul burst into the open

And AGELAOS in the act of turning
Noticed the death cloud Diomedes towering towards him
He was heaving his horses round swearing
When a spearshot pushed through his shout and out through his chest
He fell made of metal banging on the ground

Like a man put a wand of olive in the earth
And watered it and that wand became a wave
It became a whip a spine a crown
It became a wind-dictionary
It could speak in tongues
It became a wobbling wagon-load of flowers
And then a storm came spinning by

And it became a broken tree uprooted
It became a wood pile in a lonely field

Like a man put a wand of olive in the earth
And watered it and that wand became a wave
It became a whip a spine a crown
It became a wind-dictionary
It could speak in tongues
It became a wobbling wagon-load of flowers
And then a storm came spinning by
And it became a broken tree uprooted
It became a wood pile in a lonely field

Eight flint-leaved arrows seemingly out of nowhere
Shot through ORSILOCHUS
ORMENUS
OPHELESTES
DAETOR
CHROMIUS
LYCOPHONTES
AMOPAON
MELANIPPUS
That was Teucer
Ducking behind his brother's shield

And now the arrow flies through GORGYTHION
Somebody's darling son

As if it was June
A poppy being hammered by the rain
Sinks its head down
It's exactly like that
When a man's neck gives in
And the bronze calyx of his helmet
Sinks his head down

As if it was June
A poppy being hammered by the rain
Sinks its head down
It's exactly like that
When a man's neck gives in
And the bronze calyx of his helmet
Sinks his head down

Poor ARCHEPTOLEMOS
Someone was there
And the next moment no one

Like fire with its loose hair flying rushes through a city
The look of unmasked light shocks everything to rubble
And flames howl through the gaps

Like fire with its loose hair flying rushes through a city
The look of unmasked light shocks everything to rubble
And flames howl through the gaps

What was that shrill sound
Five sisters at the grave
Calling the ghost of DOLON
They remember an ugly man but quick
In a crack of light in the sweet smelling glimmer before dawn
He was caught creeping to the ships
He wore a weasel cap he was soft
Dishonest scared stooped they remember
How under a spear's eye he offered everything
All his father's money all his own
Every Trojan weakness every hope of their allies
Even the exact position of the Thracians
And the colour and size and price of the horses of Rhesus
They keep asking him why why
He gave away groaning every secret in his body
And was still pleading for his head
When his head rolled onto the mud

Like the fly the daredevil fly
Being brushed away
But busying back
The lunatic fly who loves licking
And will follow a man all day
For a nip of his blood

Like the fly the daredevil fly
Being brushed away
But busying back

The lunatic fly who loves licking
And will follow a man all day
For a nip of his blood

Recently arrived and camping apart from everyone
With weapons cleaned and layed down like cutlery
This is horrible this is some kind of bloodfeast
And beside each man his horses
Twelve anonymous Thracians were killed in their sleep
Before their ghosts had time to keep hold of their names
It was so sudden
The raw meat smell of their bodies woke up the dogs
And these were rich men
They had long smooth hair but Diomedes
Red-faced quietly like a butcher keeping up with his order
Got rid of them
And the last one RHESUS was a king
He should never have come here
Bringing over the water those huge white horses
With their chains and painted cheek guards
Extraordinary creatures almost marble but moving

Like wolves always wanting something
Thin shapes always working the hills
When a shepherd lets his flocks wander
And the weaklings bleat their fear
Within seconds wolves will appear

Like wolves always wanting something
Thin shapes always working the hills
When a shepherd lets his flocks wander
And the weaklings bleat their fear
Within seconds wolves will appear

Two more metal ornaments
Knocked down anonymous in their helmets
And when those iron heads opened
Everyone whispered listen
That was ISOS and ANTIPHOS
They used to be shepherds they were hill people
Working out of reach of the world
Those were the two boys Achilles kidnapped
Among the wolves and buzzards of Mount Ida
They said it was wonderful to be tied in creepers
And taken to the other side by that gypsy
They said he could talk to horses
They said his mother was a seal or mermaid
And he introduced them to Agamemnon
The great king of Mycenae poor fools
Who came home as proud as astronauts
And didn't want to farm any more
And went riding out to be killed by Agamemnon

Like a boat
Going into the foaming mouth of a wave

In the body of the wind
Everything vanishes
And the sailors stare at mid-air

Like a boat
Going into the foaming mouth of a wave
In the body of the wind
Everything vanishes
And the sailors stare at mid-air

Antimachus was bribed this is well known
Antimachus was a friend of Paris
Who put the case for war
He opened a door in the earth
And a whole generation entered
Including his own young sons
PEISANDER and HIPPOLOCHUS
Two dazed teenagers trotting into battle
On their father's expensive horses
And those horses those colossal death-muscles
Ramped and flared and the reins
Slipped from the boys' hands
Please take us alive they shouted
Our father is Antimachus a gentleman
He has the cost of us both in cash back at home
We could fetch it
But Agamemnon remembered

Their father was that sly old man
Who tried to murder Menelaus
Antimachus assured them
He had acted in good faith
But their ghosts said nothing

Like close to the grey sea the waiting rocks
Outstare the winds and the big waves
Running at them open-mouthed

Like close to the grey sea the waiting rocks
Outstare the winds and the big waves
Running at them open-mouthed

IPHIDAMAS a big ambitious boy
At the age of eighteen at the age of restlessness
His family crippled him with love
They gave him a flute and told him to amuse himself
In his grandfather's sheep-nibbled fields
That didn't work they gave him a bride
Poor woman lying in her new name alone
She said even on his wedding night
He seemed to be wearing armour
He kept yawning and looking far away
And by the next morning he'd vanished
Arrogant farmhand fresh from the fields
He went straight for Agamemnon

Aiming for the soft bit under the breastplate
And leaning in pushing all his violence
All his crazy impatience into the thrust
But he couldn't quite break through the belt-metal
Against all that silver the spear-tip
Simply bent like lead and he lost
Poor Iphidamas now he is only iron
Sleeping its iron sleep poor boy
Who fought for Helen for his parents' town
Far from his wife all that money wasted
A hundred cattle he gave her
A thousand sheep and goats
All that hard work feeding them wasted

Grief is black it is made of earth
It gets into the cracks in the eyes
It lodges its lump in the throat
When a man sees his brother on the ground
He goes mad he comes running out of nowhere
Lashing without looking and that was how COON died
First he wounded Agamemnon
Then he grabbed his brother's stiffened foot
And tried to drag him home shouting
Help for god's sake this is Iphidamas
Someone please help but Agamemnon
Cut off his head and that was that
Two brothers killed on the same morning by the same man

That was their daylight here finished
And their long nightshift in the underworld just beginning

Like when two winds want a wood
The south wind and the east wind
Both pull at the trees' arms
And the sound of smooth-skinned cornel whipping to and fro
And oak and ash batting long sticks together
Is a word from another world

Like when two winds want a wood
The south wind and the east wind
Both pull at the trees' arms
And the sound of smooth-skinned cornel whipping to and fro
And oak and ash batting long sticks together
Is a word from another world

ASAEUS

AUTONOOS

OPITES

DOLOPS

OPHELTIUS

AGELAOS

AESYMNUS

ORUS

HIPPONOUS

THYMBRAIUS

MOLION

Like fawns running over a field
Suddenly give up and stand
Puzzled in their heavy coats

Like fawns running over a field
Suddenly give up and stand
Puzzled in their heavy coats

Also ADRESTUS and AMPHIUS
Everyone knew they were going to die
They were the sons of Merops the prophet
He begged them to stay at home but they couldn't listen
Their own ghosts were calling them to Troy
Immaculate in clean linen
They set out together but Death
Was already walking to meet them

Like a goatherd stands on a rock
And sees a cloud blowing towards him
A black block of rain coming closer over the sea
Pushing a ripple of wind inland
He shivers and drives his flocks into a cave for shelter

Like a goatherd stands on a rock
And sees a cloud blowing towards him
A black block of rain coming closer over the sea
Pushing a ripple of wind inland
He shivers and drives his flocks into a cave for shelter

And HIPPODAMOS died

Like a traveller trudging across a plain
Who comes to a river and stands helpless
Looking down at that foamy swiftness sweeping to the sea
And takes a step back

And HYPEIROCHOS died

Like a farm boy looking after the pigs
Who tries to cross a river in a rainstorm
And gets swept away

Typical competitive pride and madness
Made AGASTRAPHUS get out of his chariot
And walk and keep walking with no back-up
No friend no horse as far as the front line
Of course he was wounded he lay dying
Thinking if only if only the mind
Was more straightforward and efficient
What was I doing thinking I could walk
Through all that iron on my own

And us
Said THOON
ENNOMUS
CHERSIDAMAS

Like a fish in the wind
Jumps right out of its knowledge
And lands on the sand

Like a fish in the wind
Jumps right out of its knowledge
And lands on the sand

Come back to your city SOCUS
Your father is a rich man a breeder of horses
And your house has deep decorated baths and long passages
But he and his brother weren't listening
Like men on wire walking over the underworld
CHAROPS died first killed by Odysseus
Then Socus who was running by now
Felt the rude punch of a spear in his back
Push through his heart and out the other side poor Socus
Trying to get away from his own ending
Ran out his last moments in fear of the next ones
But this is it now this is the mud of Troy
This is black wings coming down every evening
Bird's feathers on your face
Unmaking you mouthful by mouthful
Eating your eyes your open eyes
Which your mother should have closed

Like when the wind comes ruffling at last to sailors adrift
Trying to manage the broken springs of their muscles

And lever and lift those well-rubbed oars
Making tiny dents in the ocean

Like when the wind comes ruffling at last to sailors adrift
Trying to manage the broken springs of their muscles
And lever and lift those well-rubbed oars
Making tiny dents in the ocean

And
DORYCLES
PANDOCUS
LYSANDER
PYRASUS
PYLARTES
APISAON
All vigorous men
All vanished

Like in Autumn under the dripping wind
The earth's clothes grow heavy she can hardly stand
God rains on the roof hammering his fists down
He has had enough of violent smiling men
Now every one of us is being looked at
Under the rain's lens
Now the rivers are filling they are overfilling
There are streams sawing through hills
Cutting up the grass into islands
Everything is clattering to the sea

This is water's world
And the works of men are vanishing

Like in Autumn under the dripping wind
The earth's clothes grow heavy she can hardly stand
God rains on the roof hammering his fists down
He has had enough of violent smiling men
Now every one of us is being looked at
Under the rain's lens
Now the rivers are filling they are overfilling
There are streams sawing through hills
Cutting up the grass into islands
Everything is clattering to the sea
This is water's world
And the works of men are vanishing

DAMASOS the Trojan
Running at a man thinking kill kill
In years to come someone will find his helmet
Shaped like a real head

And PYLON
ORMENOS
HIPPOMACHOS
ANTIPHATES
MENON
IAMENOS
ORESTES

Like the war cries of cranes going south escaping the rain
Every winter the clang of their wings going over us
And the shock of their parachutes
Landing on someone else's fields

Like the war cries of cranes going south escaping the rain
Every winter the clang of their wings going over us
And the shock of their parachutes
Landing on someone else's fields

EPICLES a Southerner from sunlit Lycia
Climbed the Greek wall remembering the river
That winds between his wheatfields and his vineyards
He was knocked backwards by a rock
And sank like a diver
The light in his face went out

Like the shine of a sea swell
Lifting and flattening silently
When water makes way for the wind
And dreams of its storms
Huge waves hang in a hush
Uncertain which way to fall
Until a breeze breaks them

Like the shine of a sea swell
Lifting and flattening silently
When water makes way for the wind

And dreams of its storms
Huge waves hang in a hush
Uncertain which way to fall
Until a breeze breaks them

Honourable IMBRIOS left his house in Pedaios
And took lodgings in a drafty street in Troy
He could have been a rich man
He married Priam's daughter Medesicaste
But his marriage was a death warrant
How can you kiss a rolling head

Even AMPHIMACHOS died and he was a rarity
A green-eyed changeable man from Elis
He was related to Poseidon
You would think the sea could do something
But it just lifted and flattened lifted and flattened

Like a stone
Stands by a grave and says nothing

Like a stone
Stands by a grave and says nothing

In this love-story there was a man
Who wanted to marry Cassandra
And she was Priam's bright-eyed neurotic
Most beautiful daughter

And he was OTHRYON the dreamer
Who came from Cabesus with no money
When he offered his life for her hand
Her father accepted
And so the dreamer went blushing into battle and died
And everyone laughed and laughed
Except Cassandra

Like a deer in the hills wounded
Keeps running in pain
There are dogs following her bloodprints
But she goes on and on escaping into loneliness
To the very breaking of her being
Until it happens in some shadowy wood on a hilltop
She gives up
And the dogs set about eating her
But at last at evening a lion appears
A huge angel wandering the hills laying claim to the dead
And the dogs scatter

At last at evening a lion appears
A huge angel wandering the hills laying claim to the dead
And the dogs scatter

Oh ASIUS ASIUS how has he done this
Now he bangs down his knuckles on his knees
He feels so luminous stupid

Sitting in god's headlights trembling
In the narrow opening to the grave
He was told to dismount
And proceed on foot to the Greek camp
But he couldn't hear he couldn't stop
Having ridden those shining horses
Over the Selleis and the Simois
And all the stony way from Arisbe to Troy

Like when winnowers bang their shovels down
Black beans and chickpeas jump in the wind
Their seed-shrouds flit along the ground

Like when winnowers bang their shovels down
Black beans and chickpeas jump in the wind
Their seed-shrouds flit along the ground

Somebody's husband somebody's daughter's husband
Stood there stunned by fear
Like a pillar like a stunted tree
He couldn't bend his stones
He couldn't walk his roots
His armour was useless it simply
Cried out and broke open oh
There stood ALCATHOUS and a spear
Knowing nothing of his wedding
Not knowing his feelings or his wife's face

Or her doting parents or her incredible needlework
That spear went straight through his heart
And began to tick tick tick but not for love

Like a knife-winged hawk
Balanced on a cliff with no foothold
Not even a goat can climb there
Like when he lifts his blades and begins
That faultless fall
Through the birds of the valley

Like a knife-winged hawk
Balanced on a cliff with no foothold
Not even a goat can climb there
Like when he lifts his blades and begins
That faultless fall
Through the birds of the valley

OINOMAOS

ASKALAPHOS

APHAREUS

THOON

ANTILOCHUS

DEIPUROS

PEISANDER

HARPALION not quite ready for life
Not quite solid always shifting from foot to foot

With his eyes sliding everywhere in fear
Followed his father to war .
He never came back to that house
Three storeys high on the River Parthenios
It was horrible the death-howl
Of the father finding him gone

Like deer always moving on and looking back
Knowing they are wanted by wolves they keep
Stepping away through the pillars of the woods
Knowing their guests are waiting

Like deer always moving on and looking back
Knowing they are wanted by wolves they keep
Stepping away through the pillars of the woods
Knowing their guests are waiting

EUCHENOR a kind of suicide
Carried the darkness inside him of a dud choice
Either he could die at home of sickness
Or at Troy of a spearwound
His mother was in tears
His father was in tears but
Cold as a coin he took the second option
Seeing as otherwise he'd have had to pay a fine
It was no surprise when an arrow pierced his neck
He recognised that prick of darkness

Like a stallion tugging at a rope breaks loose at last
And his gallop is a drumbeat shaking the valley
There he goes heading straight for the river
Longing to wash in that clattering rush of cold
When he holds his head high and runs like a king
Under the wind-blown banner of his mane
Then he knows his knees are going to lift him forever
And a grassy cloth has been spread on the fields for his pleasure

Like a stallion tugging at a rope breaks loose at last
And his gallop is a drumbeat shaking the valley
There he goes heading straight for the river
Longing to wash in that clattering rush of cold
When he holds his head high and runs like a king
Under the wind-blown banner of his mane
Then he knows his knees are going to lift him forever
And a grassy cloth has been spread on the fields for his pleasure

Who could be more ordinary than SATNIUS
The son of Water
When he died the River was so cold
You'd never think it was his mother

And PROTHOENOR died

And then a spear with its own willpower
Flying towards another man

Chose to miss him at the last minute
And struck ARCHELOCHUS

Like the changing mind
That moves a cloud off a mountain
And makes rocks and cliffs appear
Pushing the landshape's sharp edges up
Through more and more air

Like the changing mind
That moves a cloud off a mountain
And makes rocks and cliffs appear
Pushing the landshape's sharp edges up
Through more and more air

Then PROMACHUS fell forgetting everything

Like when they're cutting ash poles in the hills
The treetops fall as soft as cloth

Like when they're cutting ash poles in the hills
The treetops fall as soft as cloth

ILIONEUS an only child ran out of luck
He always wore that well-off look
His parents had a sheep farm
They didn't think he would die
But a spear stuck through his eye

He sat down backwards
Trying to snatch back the light
With stretched out hands

Like oak trees swerving out of the hills
And setting their faces to the wind
Day after day being practically lifted away
They are lashed to the earth
And never let go
Gripping on darkness

Like oak trees swerving out of the hills
And setting their faces to the wind
Day after day being practically lifted away
They are lashed to the earth
And never let go
Gripping on darkness

Now STICHIUS has gone and ARCESILAUS

Like smoke leaving the earth vanishing up
When a town is under attack on a faraway island
All day in a trance of war men murder each other
But at dusk silence only the fingers of fires
Lifting their question to the mainland
Is there anybody there please help

Like smoke leaving the earth vanishing up
When a town is under attack on a faraway island
All day in a trance of war men murder each other
But at dusk silence only the fingers of fires
Lifting their question to the mainland
Is there anybody there please help

Poor wandering MEDON born out of wedlock
Stuck his hand into this ice-cold world
And didn't like it but he had no choice
Grew up in Locris under the smile
Of a slim respectable stepmother
And murdered her brother
Then it was years of sleeping under bushes
He went north to Phylace then north to Troy
And at last in the ninth year
Death kicked him and he kicked it back
He was close to no one

Like when a donkey walking by a cornfield
Decides to stop
Stands there being prodded and whacked
Thinking good I will wade and eat sideways
And does just that eats and eats sunk in a pond of corn
Exhausted farm boys beat him with sticks
Their arms ache their sticks break
But nothing moves that big lump of donkey
From the fixed statue of his eating

Until he's full and of his own iron will
Walks on

And
IASUS
MECISTEUS
ECHIUS
CLONIUS
DEIOCHUS

Like bird families feeding by a river
Hundreds of geese and herons and long-necked swans
When an ember of eagle a red hot coal of hunger
Falls out of the sky and bursts into wings

Like bird families feeding by a river
Hundreds of geese and herons and long-necked swans
When an ember of eagle a red hot coal of hunger
Falls out of the sky and bursts into wings

KALETOR carrying a flaming bit of wood
About to fling it at the ships
He and the fire went out together

And LYKOPHRON

And KLEITOS it goes on and on
His empty cart clattering away through leafless trees

And
SCHEDIOS
LAODAMAS
OTOS
KROISMOS

Like thick flocks of falling snow
In winter when god showers his arrows at us
Pouring them down putting the winds to sleep
Until the hills the headlands the grassy lowlands
All the ploughs and crops of the earth every living twig
Is wiped out white with snow it goes on and on
Falling and falling on the grey sea
Blotting out harbours and beaches
And only the breakers can shake it off endlessly rushing at the shore
That's how blank it is when the world succumbs to snow

Like thick flocks of falling snow
In winter when god showers his arrows at us

Pouring them down putting the winds to sleep
Until the hills the headlands the grassy lowlands
All the ploughs and crops of the earth every living twig
Is wiped out white with snow it goes on and on
Falling and falling on the grey sea
Blotting out harbours and beaches
And only the breakers can shake it off endlessly rushing at the shore
That's how blank it is when the world succumbs to snow

DOLOPS the strongest son of Lampus
Not believing he could die
Even when his spear hit solid metal
And banged back again
Even when a man hacked off his helmet
And he saw his own eye-holes
Staring up at him from the ground
It was not until the beak of death
Pushed out through his own chest
That he recognised the wings of darkness

Like when god unwinds his whirlwind
A single cloud moves into the middle sky

MELANIPPUS not really a fighter more a farmer

PERIPHETOS the man from Mycenae
Who tripped on his shield

Like winter rivers pouring off the mountains
The thud of water losing consciousness
When it falls down from the high places
Mixing its streams in the havoc of a valley
And far away a shepherd hears it

Like winter rivers pouring off the mountains
The thud of water losing consciousness
When it falls down from the high places
Mixing its streams in the havoc of a valley
And far away a shepherd hears it

The River Axius has the silverest sweetest water
It flows through Paeonia
Where there are bison in the hills
And men make curved bows from their horns
To get there you have to go miles over mountains
Some of his men might make it
But not PURAICHMES

Like a man running in a dream
Can never approach a man escaping
Who can never escape a man approaching

Like a man running in a dream
Can never approach a man escaping
Who can never escape a man approaching

And

AREILYCUS

THOAS

AMPHICLUS

ATUMNIOS

MARIS

KLEOBULOS

LYKON

AKAMAS

ERYMAS

PRONOOS

THESTOR

ERYLAOS

ERYMAS

AMPHOTERUS

EPALTES

TLEPOLEMOS

ECHIOS

PURIS

IPHES

EUIPPOS

POLYMELOS

THRASYMELOS

Like hawkwings cut through a sheet of starlings
Like wing-scissors open and close
Through a billow of jackdaws

Like hawkwings cut through a sheet of starlings
Like wing-scissors open and close
Through a billow of jackdaws

One side had stables and stone water troughs
They caught a horse in the windy hills
They put it in the king's paddock
And called it PEDASUS the Leaper
The other side had sacks of white barley
They stole that horse and whipped it into battle
Pedasus with unquestioning eyes
Carried and served both sides
Now the earth is his owner

Like a drop of fig juice squeezed into milk
Mysteriously thickens it
As if a drip of lethargy
Falls into the bucket
And the woman stirring
Stops

Like a drop of fig juice squeezed into milk
Mysteriously thickens it
As if a drip of lethargy
Falls into the bucket
And the woman stirring
Stops

SARPEDON the son of Zeus
Came to this ungreen ungrowing ground
Came from his cornfields from his leafy river
From his kingdom of paths and apple groves
And was killed by a spear
Then for a long time he lay crumpled as linen
Until two soft-voiced servants Sleep and Death
Carried him home again they left him
Folded on the grass and a breeze from heaven
Almost lifted him up almost shook him out
And set him sighing and whispering but no one
Not even a great man not even a son of Zeus
Can buy or steal or borrow back his own last breath
Once he has hissed it out
Through the shutter of his teeth

Like the blue flower of the sea
Being bruised by the wind
Like when the rain-wind
Bullies the warm wind
Battering the great soft sunlit clouds
Deep scoops of wind
Work the sea into a wave
And foam follows wandering gusts
A thousand feet high

Like the blue flower of the sea
Being bruised by the wind

Like when the rain-wind
Bullies the warm wind
Battering the great soft sunlit clouds
Deep scoops of wind
Work the sea into a wave
And foam follows wandering gusts
A thousand feet high

One of the Myrmidons a man of influence
A prince of Budeion he was well-dressed
He was generous and reliable
Until he killed his cousin
Then he became a runaway then a beggar
Then a soldier then a corpse
A sharp rock struck him
And the understanding drained from his skull
Now he doesn't recognise himself
He seems paler than EPIGEUS

Like anger which is so rapturous so other
It can turn a man any man into a murderer
Then all his learning is outwitted
He has to leave his home his country
And go begging for shelter
With blood printed on his hands
And wherever he goes
People stare and whisper

Like anger which is so rapturous so other
It can turn a man any man into a murderer
Then all his learning is outwitted
He has to leave his home his country
And go begging for shelter
With blood printed on his hands
And wherever he goes
People stare and whisper

BATHYCLES and LAOGONUS
One a rich man one a priest
Both became earth

In a courtyard on a flat stone
Two children were playing dice
And a quarrel had broken out
Women rushed to the door
They saw one child kill the other
That was PATROCLUS nicknamed Innocent
Who grew up blurred under the background noise
Of his foster-brother's voice
And borrowed his armour
In the mess of war he forgot his instructions
He kept killing and killing
Until the crack of his spear splintering
And the hush of his helmet spinning through the air
And the rare and immediate light

Of Apollo with one hand
Stopped him

Like moonlight
Or the light of a bonfire
Burning on the cliffs
When sailors get blown along
Homesick over the sea
They notice that far-off fire
And think of their wives

Like moonlight
Or the light of a bonfire
Burning on the cliffs
When sailors get blown along
Homesick over the sea
They notice that far-off fire
And think of their wives

EUPHORBAS died
Leaving his silver hairclip on the battlefield

And HIPPOTHOUS
SCHEDIUS
PHORCYS
LEOCRITUS

Like little campfire stars lit round the moon
No wind at all
Under an upturned glass of air
Exact black rocks show clear
And the world simplifies into cliffs and clefts
On nights like this
Light is unspeakable it is breaking out of heaven
And every star openly admits to god
Making the shepherd glad

Like little campfire stars lit round the moon
No wind at all
Under an upturned glass of air
Exact black rocks show clear
And the world simplifies into cliffs and clefts
On nights like this
Light is unspeakable it is breaking out of heaven
And every star openly admits to god
Making the shepherd glad

APISAON
ARETUS

PODES a close friend of Hector
They used to have meals together
He panicked he tried to run back to those times
But time itself finished him

Like fire which is what
A kind of visible vanishing
That lights up trees
The wind whisks it round
It is nothing it is exhausting
Whole thickets lose their footing and fall
Under the weight of that light

Like fire which is what
A kind of visible vanishing
That lights up trees
The wind whisks it round
It is nothing it is exhausting
Whole thickets lose their footing and fall
Under the weight of that light

And KOIRANUS who came from the bright chalk cliffs
Of Crete he was a quiet man
A light to his loved ones

And IPHITUS who was born in the snow
Between two tumbling trout-stocked rivers
Died on the flat dust
Not far from DEMOLEON and HIPPODAMAS

Like when a dolphin powered by hunger
Swims into the harbour
Thousands of light-storms of little fish

Flit away to the water-shaken wall-shadow
And hang there trembling

Like when a dolphin powered by hunger
Swims into the harbour
Thousands of light-storms of little fish
Flit away to the water-shaken wall-shadow
And hang there trembling

POLYDORUS is dead who loved running
Now somebody has to tell his father
That exhausted man leaning on the wall
Looking for his favourite son

Like a lion leading his cubs through a wood
Walks into a line of huntsmen
And stares himself stronger
Clenching his whole face fistlike
Around the stones of his eyes

Like a lion leading his cubs through a wood
Walks into a line of huntsmen
And stares himself stronger
Clenching his whole face fistlike
Around the stones of his eyes

There lay DRYOPS

Like that dog in the barn
Lying in a darkless half-sleep guarding his sheep
All night there's a lump of growl stuck in his throat
So the fox tip-toeing through the woods
Worries him awake

Like that dog in the barn
Lying in a darkless half-sleep guarding his sheep
All night there's a lump of growl stuck in his throat
So the fox tip-toeing through the woods
Worries him awake

And DEMUCHUS
LAOGONUS
DARDANUS

And TROS begging for his life
But his life was over

Like when two animals have found a little luckiness
Of clear-running water in the mountains
One dies and the other drinks it

Like when two animals have found a little luckiness
Of clear-running water in the mountains
One dies and the other drinks it

And MULIUS and RHIGMOS

Like on a long beach the rustle of the sea
Opening its multiple folds unfurling waves

Like on a long beach the rustle of the sea
Opening its multiple folds unfurling waves

Laothoë one of Priam's wives
Never saw her son again he was washed away
Now she can't look at the sea she can't think about
The bits unburied being eaten by fishes
He was the tall one the conscientious one
Who stayed out late pruning his father's fig trees
Who was kidnapped who was ransomed
Who walked home barefoot from Arisbe
And rested for twelve days and was killed
LYCAON killed Lycaon unkilled Lycaon
Bending down branches to make wheels
Lycaon kidnapped Lycaon pruning by moonlight
Lycaon naked in a river pleading for his life
Being answered by Achilles No

Like when a lion comes back to a forest's secret rooms
Too late
The hunter has taken her children
She follows the tracks of that man
Into every valley
With her heart's darkness
Growing darker

Like when a lion comes back to a forest's secret rooms
Too late
The hunter has taken her children
She follows the tracks of that man
Into every valley
With her heart's darkness
Growing darker

Near the old fig tree the cart track
That runs downhill from windy Troy
Passes two springs where the Scamander
Bubbles over stones the first one warm
The second one ice cold even in summer
Town people come and wash their clothes
In those smooth rock-scooped pools
The river knows their voices
But Achilles killed so many men
Standing downstream with his rude sword
Hacking off heads until the water
Burst out in anger lifting up a ridge of waves
That now this whole river is a grave
Women at the washing pools
When they hear the river running
Crying like a human through its chambers
They remember THERSILOCHUS lying
In a quick-moving never-ending darkness
Between steep steps of echoing rocks
They remember MYDON that frightened face

Falling out of sight under the tamarisks
And ASTYPYLOS blocking the channel
MNESIUS rolled in sand THRASIUS lost in silt
AINIOS turning somersaults in a black pool
Upside down among the licking fishes
And OPHELESTES his last breath silvering the surface
All that beautiful armour underwater
All those white bones sunk in mud
And instead of a burial a wagtail
Sipping the desecration unaware

Like when a man dives off a boat
Into wind-blackened water
He vanishes then surfaces
With his thoughts the other way up
And his hands full of oysters

Like when a man dives off a boat
Into wind-blackened water
He vanishes then surfaces
With his thoughts the other way up
And his hands full of oysters

And HECTOR died like everyone else
He was in charge of the Trojans
But a spear found out the little patch of white
Between his collarbone and his throat
Just exactly where a man's soul sits

Waiting for the mouth to open
He always knew it would happen
He who was so boastful and anxious
And used to nip home deafened by weapons
To stand in full armour in the doorway
Like a man rushing in leaving his motorbike running
All women loved him
His wife was Andromache
One day he looked at her quietly
He said I know what will happen
And an image stared at him of himself dead
And her in Argos weaving for some foreign woman
He blinked and went back to his work
Hector loved Andromache
But in the end he let her face slide from his mind
He came back to her sightless
Strengthless expressionless
Asking only to be washed and burned
And his bones wrapped in soft cloths
And returned to the ground

Like leaves who could write a history of leaves
The wind blows their ghosts to the ground
And the spring breathes new leaf into the woods
Thousands of names thousands of leaves
When you remember them remember this
Dead bodies are their lineage
Which matter no more than the leaves

Like chaff flying everywhere at threshing time
The winnowers waft their fans and the wind does its work
And a goddess is there picking the grain from its husk
While a fine white dust covers everything

Like thousands of water birds mill and mass in the air
Great gatherings of geese and cranes and long-necked swans
Flaring and settling in those fields where the rain runs down
                                        to the Cayster
Continually shuffling and lifting and loving the sound of their wings
They shriek as they land like a huge birdfair a valleyful of voices

Like wandering tribes of flies that gather in sheds
In shadowy spring when the milk splashes in the buckets

Like crickets leaning on their elbows in the hedges
Tiny dried up men speaking pure light

Like strobe-lit wasps
That have built their nest on a footpath
Never give up their hollow house
But hang about the walls
Worrying for their children

Like tribes of summer bees
Coming up from the underworld out of a crack in a rock
A billion factory women flying to their flower work
Being born and reborn and shimmering over fields

Like locusts lifted rippling over fields on fire
Fleeing to the river
A hanging banner of insects trying to outfly flame
They hide by drowning

Like restless wolves never run out of hunger
Can eat a whole stag
Can drink the whole surface off a pool
Lapping away its blackness with thin tongues
And belching it back as blood
And still go on killing and killing
With their stomachs rubbing their sides
Haunted by hunger

Like when water hits a rocky dam
Its long strong arms can't break those stones
And all its pouring rush curls back on itself
And bleeds sideways into marshes

Like when god throws a star
And everyone looks up
To see that whip of sparks
And then it's gone

Like when god throws a star
And everyone looks up
To see that whip of sparks
And then it's gone

Afterword

Alice Oswald begins her luminous poem *Memorial* with two hundred names. As the work unfolds, these names follow their owners into the hullabaloo and upset of war. Each one comes with a nanosecond's visibility, a camera flash of passionate lyric. For a brief moment – too soon to know them, but long enough to mourn them – we see these young men leaping, screaming, running forward into dust and confusion.

And as fast as they go by, with just that speed Oswald cuts their moment into a keen, contemporary freshness of language. Here for instance is Diomedes, dealing with corpses on the battlefield 'Red faced, quietly like a butcher keeping up with his order'. Or Pandarus, furious with himself for being in the war at all. If he ever gets home, he thinks, to his wife and his 'high-roofed house', he 'will smash this bow / and throw it with my own hands into the fire'.

Now more men, more moments. All are lit by Oswald's signature alloy of diction, both hip and oracular. Soldier after soldier goes by. And however dismayed by their fate, every reader can relish the sheer verve of language that conveys it. In a few searing lines each name joins a young man, until all of them stand in front of us. Here's Pylaemenes, whose 'heart was made of coarse cloth' and whose 'manners were loose like old sacking'. And Iphidamus, a 'big, ambitious boy', so determined to fight that even on his wedding night his new bride thought 'he seemed to be wearing armour'. And Echepolus who died 'letting the darkness leak down over his eyes'.

All of them are moving in one direction. All the names, neatly cataloged in the first pages of this poem, are following their owners into oblivion. They will all die in front of us before the poem is over. And we shouldn't be surprised. There can be no other ending. In fact, they have already died long ago. They have already been named by Homer in the *Iliad*. Now Alice Oswald names them again.

Memorial is built on Homer's *Iliad*. It stands squarely on an epic foundation. The names are the same. Some of the actions are the same. The locations are identical. The similes are comparable. But why, the reader might ask, do these young men need to die again? Didn't Homer already lay them down in his great text?

These questions, far from being unsettling, are exciting. As are the clues Oswald offers in her preface. Despite her strong background as a classicist and her plain love for Homer's epic, she is candid about taking liberties. 'My approach to translation,' she writes, 'is fairly irreverent. I work closely with the Greek, but instead of carrying the words over into English, I use them as openings through which to see what Homer was looking at.'

Oswald acknowledges the *Iliad* as debt and detour. 'This is a translation of the *Iliad*'s atmosphere, not its story.' She speaks of stripping away narrative, and this purposeful reductiveness clarifies our view. Through it we can look freshly, to paraphrase her, at what Homer was looking at. And what we see there is remarkable.

What we see above all is that the atmosphere of epic has no expiry date. The soldiers here are not ciphers any more than they are merely symbols in the *Iliad*. In fact, the opposite is true. They are the brothers, husbands, sons of every war. And as we put down *Memorial* we wonder whether we first met them in Homer's epic or saw them on last night's news bulletin.

II

Alice Oswald describes *Memorial* as an 'excavation of the *Iliad*'. In her preface she places herself in the active role of oral inheritor, rather than the more passive one of translator. 'I write through the Greek, not from it – aiming for translucence rather than translation,' she states. 'I think this method, as well as my reckless dismissal of seven-eighths of the poem, is compatible with the spirit of oral poetry, which was never stable but always adapting itself to a new audience, as if its language, unlike written language, was still alive and kicking.'

The spirit of oral poetry is everywhere in *Memorial*. In the catalogs, in the cadences, but especially in Oswald's decision that her method should remove 'narrative, as you might lift the roof off a church in order to remember what you're worshipping'. After that, she writes, 'What's left is a bipolar poem made of similes and short biographies of soldiers'.

It is the similes juxtaposed to the biographies that make the reader part of the action. Oswald lays the lyric world beside violent death, like someone putting summer flowers in a coffin: a reminder of all that's been lost. In one compelling passage, the death of a soldier, Scamandrius, is paired with a haunting simile of childhood. The graphic violence of his end – 'One spear-thrust through the shoulders / And the point came out through the ribs' – is framed by an animated sketch of a small, yearning child. The pairing is unforgettable.

> Like when a mother is rushing
> And a little girl clings to her clothes
> Wants help wants arms
> Won't let her walk
> Like staring up at that tower of adulthood
> Wanting to be light again
> Wanting this whole problem of living to be lifted
> And carried on a hip

These similes also allow Oswald to use one of the most compelling strategies in this book. The biography of each dead and dying soldier is followed by a simile. The similes occur in short stanzas like the one above, mentioning woodlands, children, sunlight, locales. These in turn serve to widen the blunt record of death into the music of elegy. They help to get at that essence of epic on which Oswald is so obviously focused. But just as we take this in, just as we absorb the juxtaposition, the simile-stanza is repeated. In fact, every simile-stanza occurs twice, right through the poem. The effect is intense. The soldiers die in one paragraph, but the world they lose occurs in two. The repeated stanzas hold an acoustic mirror up to each other. The repetition builds throughout the poem into a sheer persuasion of sound. Look, it seems to say, the ruin and music of war are sensory, not logical. Here for instance is Phaestus from Tarne:

> What happened to Phaestus
> He came from Tarne where the soil is loose and crumbly
>
> Like snow falling like snow
> When the living winds shake the clouds into pieces
> Like flutters of silence hurrying down
> To put a stop to the earth at her leafwork
>
> Like snow falling like snow
> When the living winds shake the clouds into pieces
> Like flutters of silence hurrying down
> To put a stop to the earth at her leafwork.

This bold practice aligns *Memorial* even more with the old, sacred purpose of the oral tradition, which is nothing less than to be an understudy for human memory. It is this which makes *Memorial* — in Oswald's eloquent phrase — 'an oral cemetery'.

III

Of all the conversations that have sustained poetry in the last half century, few are as rich or exciting as the one about poetic translation. *Memorial* enters this conversation at a steep angle, sparking fresh insight and questions. We can see it evokes the *Iliad*. But what exactly does this evocation mean in our time and for it? How are we to read the relation between the two poems? Is *Memorial* a translation, an interpretation, or a restatement? A response? Certainly its originality suggests that it can't be categorized.

The source is clear. The *Iliad* is the story of the Trojan War. Its composition has been located in the eighth century, although controversy about the date remains. In the narrative, the Greeks, or Achaeans, wage war against the city of Troy because one of its princes has stolen Helen, the wife of the Spartan king, Menelaus. The *Iliad* remains one of the most compelling works in the Western canon – a mysterious alchemy of a possibly historical war and fictional gods.

If the story of the *Iliad* is hard to extract from myth, its poet is even more shadowy. We have assumed him to be a single poet, but there is controversy about that, too. The few legends we have are unreliable. Some of them may have been smuggled out of folkloric texts that belong to Homer's time but were probably the work of many poets. There is a reference to a blind Aeolian poet; there is a mention of Smyrna. But the connections are hard to prove. Across time, details have remained scarce and hard to come by. The truth is, Homer signals to us from a vast achievement, with no indulgence at all for our age of autobiography.

But one thing we do know; one thing we can hold on to. And it has everything to do with the relation between these two poems: the *Iliad* – at least in its original form –was recited or sung, not written. Scholars have long accepted that it is an oral composition, reaching down into the patterned words of a preliterate culture, dipping its similes and images into a deep well of musical and memorable speech.

The Greek poet Pindar, who lived a few hundred years after Homer's time, referred to such a composition as a 'rhapsode' and its creator as 'a rhapsodist', although that term was not used in Homer's time. There is even a hint that the rhapsodist held a wand in his hand as he began his recitation, just as the Anglo-Saxon scop recited *Beowulf* accompanied by a harp. In the same way, not so long ago, a traditional singer in the West of Ireland would have a man stand behind him as he sang unaccompanied, moving the singer's arm to the beat of the song. Ancient methods of keeping time. Ancient ways of measuring the world.

The most important fact in all this, the one essential to understanding the relation between *Memorial* and the *Iliad* is in the nature of both poems: A written text is fixed. An oral composition is not. There is a splendid air of unfinished business about an oral poem. And until it was written down and standardized, it's not unreasonable to imagine that the reciter of the *Iliad* might well have intervened in the poem, adding and embellishing. For the reader of a later age, living in an era of fixed text, there is something bright and moving in this image of the *Iliad* as a river, not an inland sea, flowing in and out of song, performance, memory, elegy and human interaction.

The best way of seeing *Memorial,* and its relationship to the *Iliad,* may be right here. As an evocation of a living, fluid tradition, an ardent remaking of a poem that was almost certainly hospitable to new makers in its origin. Seen this way, as an extension of rich and ancient improvisations, *Memorial* has a subtle and respectful relation to the *Iliad*, but by no means a submissive one.

Within that relation, the poem enacts the quality Oswald points to her in her preface. 'Matthew Arnold (and almost everyone ever since),' she says there, 'has praised the *Iliad* for its "nobility". But ancient critics praised its *"enargeia"*, which means something like "bright unbearable reality". ' It is this reality we track as readers of *Memorial*, as we note the names, unite them to their owners and join both to their similes. And as we follow them to the end, we can watch this reworking of an ancient epic unfold in front of us into one of the most tender-hearted and ambitious of contemporary poems.

Eavan Boland